I0756596

POT OF QUOTES, THOUGHTS AND IDEAS

Soul Food for Wealthy Living

OLATUNDE ODEYEMI

Copyright © 2020 by Olatunde Odeyemi

ISBN: 9798605834946

Independently Published

All rights reserved. All quotes in this book are originally authored by Olatunde Odeyemi.

Except for brief quotations in a review, no part of this book may be reproduced or transmitted in any form without the prior written consent of the author.

Cover Photo Credit: Pixabay.com

Published in the United States of America

Dedication

Dedicated for all to be educated!

To the one who believes and receives in feeding the soul of the mind and not just the stomach so there is no hunger for life but only fullness of life and more life.

To the "omnipotent potentials" calling for expression from inside of you to the manifestation on the outside of you even to the ends of the earth without any limitations.

For you to discover that you are a "living legend and a legacy" in this body and not merely created as a "leg on each end" of this body!

Introduction

This book is written for you to multiply your life with these simple but highly transformative quotes, thoughts and ideas!

I could have chosen not to write this book with the excuse that there's an infinite number of books in existence already. Is the universe complaining that there's no room to store all the books that are still going to be published? There's enough room for every book to be stored including your books, and the books that will be published in the next century or the next millennium and beyond!

There's more than enough room for every idea with your name on it, even amid all other similar ideas! That's why you have a name so it can be tagged on your invention or legacy!

I encourage you to discontinue every excuse about bringing your invention to life because you think someone else has already done it! You can do it, do it and let it be a story in history that you did it, it was done and there was none like it because there's no one like you!

As you become intentional in continuously fulfilling the highest potential from within, beware of the company around you!

When I published my first book and was very excited to show a friend of mine, I was disappointed by my friend's remarks.

My friend mocked me outrightly by saying with a very big laugh: "Do you ever think you can make the best-selling list in the next ten years?" I don't know if you've ever experienced a glass of cold water thrown on your face on a very cold day? That's how I felt for a second. I took a deep long breath before responding with the affirmation:

"I am going global because my gifts will make a way for me; right now, let me use my energy to keep going instead of trying to convince you."

From the word- opinion, you find the words- onion and pin. I'm not surprised when people give an opinion and it just smells like onion or it feels like a pin. That doesn't mean I will rub onion over my body or stick myself with a pin! It's just your opinion, dear friend!

My friend's opinion could have deterred my other successes by making me shrink to the level of inferiority and impossibility that was hilariously suggested to me.

A person's opinion cannot make me doubt the divine talents that are grafted in me by my maker.

I refuse to be upset in the journey of prosperity and continue to build my "peace up" to avoid being "pissed off" by anyone!

How many of us have made excuses that we could not get to a certain height in life because of what someone said to us many years ago? That is an expired lie! Get inspired by the truth of greatness that is breathing inside of you as you transform your life from now on, whether you are young, middle-aged, or old!

Give an immediate silent eviction to any opinion of condemnation that brings no liberation! There's NO need to argue with anyone. You can nod your head in silence to what another person has to say and then say NO loudly in your heart, to save you the headache from an argument. Let your last argument be the last time you beat yourself up in the wasteful effort of trying to prove a point. Make your life a focus that proves the point! Do you ever hear of the sun or the moon shouting when taking their quiet spot to display their global radiance? NO! So, why argue?

1. I will see no limitation; I will become no imitation because in my imagination there is a nation. That is the revelation for my transformation and reformation!

2. A person with a purpose is like the invisible sunlight at midnight with certainty that the morning shall make its call for its bright light. This means it is inevitable!

3. Tune in to a life of purpose, it's beautiful beyond any color that you predicted and can make a rainbow out of your darkest colors!

4. You've been given a paintbrush by the creator to paint the glory of your life with your abilities, talents, and gifts. Start painting colorfully!

5. The purpose of your life is ambiguous beyond ambition so don't live on a narrow lane of ambition! Expand your horizon with a purpose and not a position!

6. This is a personal question, or you can take it personally. "Who are you?" "Who do you think you are?" This is a personal discussion!

7. When you look in the mirror, do you see yourself or someone else? Don't convince yourself to be someone else! You are awesome!

8. Please let me be! Nobody permits you to be yourself so there's no need pleading to be you. You just are! Just be you! Be you!

9. Life allowed you to be great and grateful since the day you were born, perhaps you were never ready. It's not too late if you start being great and grateful NOW!

10. You can pay a surgeon to fix the scars of your body but you cannot get a surgeon to fix your mind. I pray today for divine healing for all humans in their body, spirit, soul, mind, thoughts, words, ways, and all of their days!

11. If you are waiting for someone to make you happy, you may have to wait until eternity. Instead of waiting for happiness, turn to happiness right **NOW!** Don't make your happiness the sole responsibility of others but yours! Tune in to happiness as the clock ticks **NOW!**

12. A happy new year means the calendar changed automatically but did you change intentionally? Be the happy new you this moment without waiting for January 1 to permit you! This moment is your January 1.

13. From the first day of a new year until a few weeks after, each person recites or receives the affirmation- "happy new year" at least a hundred times. So why not make the best of it and truly affirm a happy new year with your life? Be happy! Be new! It's that simple!

14. Never be apologetic for being hopeful and joyful. If someone is offended because of your positive emission, the person can take the case to the Supreme court! Guess what? The case will be ruled in your favor because the judge will sentence the person to a lifetime of new hope and joy, just like you!

15. A conversation between two people: "Why are you always smiling and laughing as if you don't have problems?" The response: "Get busy doing a case study on my non-existing problems or join me in the existing laughter solution!"

16. I searched and researched for the **medication** that would cure my mind of fear and failure. I could not find it so I created the **mindcation** for renewing my mind with faith to build a successful future starting NOW!

17. I also searched the store for a mind sanitizer but could only find a hand sanitizer. I had to become my own mind sanitizer, sanitizing my mind with positive thoughts and eliminating every negative thought before germinating!

18. Are you dedicated to your television or your vision in life? Television is a vision someone else created for you to watch! What is the vision you have for others to watch? You are banned from watching the television until you discover your vision!

19. What is your mission in life? When you have a mission, you become a transmission for a vision of aspiration without expiration. You discover your intention to be the continuation of inspiration and innovation for the preparation of the next generation starting **NOW!**

20. We were all endowed with the possibilities of being our best. The choice is ours to walk in those created possibilities or to recreate impossibilities. Nobody is paid to dream for you. Failure is not an excuse to denounce or renounce success. Failure is a pointer that you are on the path of success!

21. Success means to keep going blissfully without knocking others down but instead lifting others as you ride to the ends of the earth with heavenly speed. Success is not arrogant neither is it ignorant!

22. When your intuition, intention and instruction are in sync, the obstruction must sink for the construction of your miracles!

23. It's okay to doubt that the best will happen, but still, do your best to "doubt the doubt" that nothing but the best will happen.

24. In the word- restlessness, you find the word- rest. Will you seek rest or restlessness? How about making a story from the word- history, in your world?

25. Stop judging others with your words and actions! If you want to be a judge, do it the right way. Enroll in college for a law degree, pass the exams and then practice as a judge after serving as a lawyer. This should take you at least seven years to complete the steps to becoming a judge. For now, don't do it the cheap way!

26. Do not break people with your hard words like wood, but bake them with your soft words like adding sugar to a sweet cake mix in the process. I'm not talking about flattery but buttery!

27. You can either decide to be a flower or a thorn to others. If you decide to be a thorn, first of all, get a real thorn to prick yourself and see how it feels! Do you promise to become a flower? **YES!**

28. Once I met two people with a negative attitude but did not give up on them growing into a positive attitude. Didn't the mathematician say (negative x negative = positive)? Do you know anyone who has a negative attitude? Don't give up on such a person. Do your best to keep on being an example of positivity in our world. Thank you!

29. Be the ambassador of sunshine to humanity! How about making the job of the sun easier today by taking a little of the sunshine with you to brighten everyone you see and everywhere you go? On behalf of the sun, I'm saying thank you in advance!

30. The world does not need any more earthquakes. Are you living your life as a natural disaster or a natural enhancer to those around you? Don't be the weather that pisses everyone off! Please become a rain of peace! Please! Peace!

31. A young child heard the word FLU and immediately shouted: F for Friendship, L for Love, and U for Understanding! Yes, I have the FLU! Everyone needs Friendship, Love, and Understanding. FLU!

32. Your life is a job that you must work overtime on to create more values which will eventually yield more in the bank of life. When was the last time you worked overtime on yourself by reading a book, attended a seminar or webinar, listened to a mentor, or sat down all night to write a business plan?

33. Sometimes in life, we think we have to convince people to believe in our greatness because of our present circumstances. Beware of trying to convince people about the certainty of your destiny with intensity! Convince only yourself!

34. How are you running your race in the field of life? Are you flying like an eagle or waddling like a duck? Are you sprinting like a lion or scurrying like a mouse? Fly with the courage and conviction of an eagle and then move to another level of flying by soaring forever!

35. Don't limit your One to None. One can become One hundred. One hundred can become One thousand. One thousand can become One hundred thousand. One hundred thousand can become One million and more. What is your One, dearest one?

36. Work on that million-dollar idea even if it generates just a dollar today. Turn your discouragement to encouragement and don't stop working on that million-dollar idea. Eventually, you'll be laughing in million-dollar returns! **Believe and Receive your million dollars!**

37. Don't crunch your hunch of ideas but launch it, for it may lead you to the brunch or lunch of blessings in the plate on that first date with success without stress!

38. Once I had a friend who did not believe in God. Each time my friend had a problem the first words to be uttered were: "Oh, my God!" I discovered a lesson that it's okay to have a "belief" in your "unbelief" as long as you "believe". I'm sure, it's not only my friend that exclaims: "Oh, my God!" when confronted with fear or faith.

39. Sometimes, I try to imagine the creation of heaven and earth, the first human being on earth, the first house, the creation of all the roads in the world, all the airplanes flying around the world... And I scream STOP! Accept it all in faith.

40. When life gets complicated, don't get cremated with the complaints! All you can do to get sedated is to breathe in with lungs of gratitude. Inhaling gratitude and exhaling stress, serve the role of a tranquilizer at the sole of your soul!

41. Do you believe in self-talk and prayer? Begin to swim in the deepest parts of your heart by allowing your words and silence to send waves to the temple of your soul. Have you prayed today?

42. Prayer is an extra layer we can all afford to wear. Life can get cold despite the extra layers of blankets and sweaters, but don't forget that prayer is an extra layer that you can always add to the extra layers without being weighed down. And when life gets hot, change the garment of your prayer! All is well!

43. **Retirement** sounds like a life sentence to permanent tiredness. I just wonder why it was never called **restrengthenment** - a time for new strength to live another phase of life, still doing your best!

44. Don't get tired in the business of life so you don't get fired. Get inspired! It's a new day to be hired again with the purposeful resume of productivity and prosperity! You are the most wanted candidate for mega-size dreams that become reality! Renew your mentality!

45. As you keep ascending the mountains of success, never allow your character to descend. Your character is your most important survival kit on the mountain top.

46. When you climb the ladder of success into the sky, don't throw a handful of dust from above on those who held the ladder steadily for you as you climbed upwards. Remember to send them a handful of gratitude from your altitude!

47. Life does not open up to us as we move about busily at the speed of an airplane but as we slow down and trail the path of quietness like the turtle. Slow down, NOW!

48. **Meditation** is a **medication** that I give to myself twice daily or as often as needed. There is no overdosing in this self-prescription of meditation to combat all manipulations of the mind.

49. You should receive a citation for no meditation. Don't wait for a conviction before meditation. Just meditate! Get quiet! Be still!

50. **Mind-fullness** comes before **mouth-fullness**. Before you open your mouth, check in with your mind before your words spill out! How many times have you heard people say: "How I wish I never said that?" Don't be one of those who never stop one moment to think before they talk!

51. Treat each person with the utmost respect whether a beggar or royalty. Learn the theory of respect and fairness to all from the air we breathe. Fresh air is given in the same proportion to the peasant and the president!

52. Don't refer to anyone as a fool. A fool today can become a full-time king or queen tomorrow. So, think twice whenever you tag someone with a label that does not dignify! Zip up inglorious titles!

53. Silence is not only the best answer for a fool, it is also the best quiz that the wise need to continuously love to solve. Silence is the recommended lens for listening. Anytime we keep acting a fool by talking endlessly, or worrying meaninglessly; we need the tool of silence!!! **SILENCE!**

54. Let your life overflow with gratitude in such a way that if a thermometer was placed on you, it would display as: "forever hot in gratitude fever." Forever grateful!

55. It's **gratitude** and not **ratitude!** **Gratitude** is a great attitude from the heart of thankfulness! **Ratitude** is **(a rat-attitude)** that sneaks to eat in an overflowing pantry without showing gratitude. If you've been living in **ratitude,** it's time to switch to gratitude **NOW! Guess** what? **I** believe you are clad in gratitude and **ratitude** will learn from you!

56. Are you grateful or ungrateful? Are you one of those people that have over ten thousand reasons why today is not a good day? Get a restraining order from the police against the complaining, ungrateful and irritable soul!

57. Poverty and prosperity are two words that you can either write with the story of your life. Pick your pen right now to cancel poverty and replace it with prosperity on the paper of your life. What are you waiting for? Pick your pen, **NOW!** Write the essay on prosperity with your life for the world to read!

58. Once I heard someone praying for money to drop from heaven as a miracle. I asked: "Wouldn't you be frightened if money suddenly dropped from the sky into your lap?" Ideas will drop from heaven and money will crawl from the earth into your bank account, when you work and walk on the ideas that are tucked away in you.

59. Attention attracts connection and direction through inspiration. What are you paying attention to? Attention spins the attraction for the creation cycle of manifestation!

60. Study the lives of successful people today so that you can have a glimpse of your own life in the book of tomorrow. You have the opportunity to edit the book of your success starting **NOW!**

61. If you are behind others today, it's a preparation for you to lead others tomorrow on the front line of success, so you make the best of today by preparing for tomorrow.

62. Learn from the losses of yesterday and earn profits on them today in the business of wisdom and knowledge for everyday living.

63. It's very easy to make gossip juice or idleness sandwich but there's no nutritional value to your soul from such recipes. Discover a new menu for positive thinking and prosperity to feed your soul!

64. Joy is a toy that's found in every living soul. You can either play with it or refuse to notice it. Play and share your **toy of joy** with others. You'll be surprised to discover that some people cannot notice joy even though it's jumping at the center of their souls! Transfer the **toy of joy** to everyone you come across on this joyful day!

65. Your income is not only the wages you earn but also everything that comes into your life. Be careful because your income will produce your outcome. What is your income? Books, ideas, gossip, healthy habits, or whatever it is. Your outcome will tell!

66. Change is usually measured on the outside by nice clothes, luxury cars, or magnificent houses. How is change measured on your inside? You cannot be great on the outside and gross on the inside! Likewise, you cannot be gross on the inside and great on the outside!

67. Mastery comes with slavery. When you become a slave to your virtues such as discipline and honesty, you eventually become a master over debt and humanity.

68. Character is the only movie in life where you are the main character. Remember that the whole world is watching you daily in this premiere of you! What does your character reveal?

69. Integrity is as insignificant as not picking your nose with your bare fingers even when you are the only audience in your bedroom!

70. You must trim your dream "every now and then" to keep it in shape! You must also give your dream the freedom to elevate, enlarge, and expand without room to contain it!

71. Life may seem to be one thing or another but just ensure you are ALL you need to be in life. "Don't be a hole in the ground view when you can be whole in the grand view." Be like an oyster recoiling into your shell and then come out as a butterfly, dazzling everyone with the radiant energy of your wings!

72. Multiply your thoughts and ideas to produce immensely and infinitely for the vicinity of the whole earth. The ideas in you are too big to be about your life alone. You are destined to make an impact on the entire universe!

73. When you receive an idea; dance with it, sing with it, paint with it, cook with it, run with it, or do something with it. There's no other day than to do something with your idea but today! Start NOW! Your best life begins with an atom of an idea that gradually becomes a national and global phenomenon!

74. Remember to guard your dream safely because it is a precious treasure that you cannot afford to drop on the road of life! If you lost the shadow of silver yesterday, don't deny yourself the light of gold in this new day!

75. Let go of lost opportunities! Crying over the lost opportunities of yesterday will not add more water to the Atlantic Ocean or the Pacific Ocean! Take off the crying mask and set a task to aim better for the stakes of today! Move on!

76. There is never a time to get ready and dressed up to meet opportunity, you just have to be ready at all times whether you are ready or not. Meet opportunity even in your sleep, NOW!

77. Regard and regrade your idea and don't disregard and degrade your idea! Your idea is the guard that will guide you as you abide in the tide!

78. Don't clean out your idea with the trash of life, ink out your idea in the stash of life, and then cash it for life!

79. You can take the stage at any age! Don't make that cheap excuse that you are too young or too old to get on the stage of greatness! The world is still waiting for your performance at any age on the stage, so come out of your cage!

80. Every human being is a potential author that can autograph the book called **LIFE** with their legacies for all to read. Your life of unlimited greatness and exploits! Your life of overflowing ideas and unstoppable possibilities! Your life of amazing accomplishments!

81. Your ideas are the greatest inheritance that you owe yourself! Nobody owes you an inheritance! Begin to nurture your ideas to manifestation and continuation for even generations not yet born!

82. Step away from the crowd at the overcrowded shallow edge! Dive into the depth of distinction! You are an uncommon and unusual human being created to recreate history with your story and the everlasting signature of your name on the map of the earth! Say goodbye to mediocrity, NOW!

83. Is the universe complaining that it is being choked with too many inventions? Start complying with the manifestation of greatness! Add your name to the list of greatness! What is your name?

84. You achieve your dream of becoming a president the day you recognize that your life is a nation that you are leading! If you preside over your life successfully, then you have won a presidency that needs no political party or election! The only campaign required is the determination without termination of inspiration in your heart!

85. If your dream was to become a pilot and you ended up as a cab driver, don't give up on life! Give that cab driver job your best energy, attitude, and excellence; because very soon that cab will grow wings and you will be flying it around the world like an airplane.

86. Your plans will help you stay grounded and your dreams will help you fly above the ground. You need both plans and dreams to create miracles! Miracles are the dreams and goals that are on the inside of every human being crying to be set free from imprisonment!

87. You don't have to get to the airport before you take your next vacation. **R**ight now, close your eyes and imagine yourself in any part of the world in the best hotel and having a fabulous time. **D**id you have to pay for it? **NO!** If you want to travel far in life, you must learn to first travel in your mind. Travel far and wide in your mind at any time and very soon, you will begin to travel far and wide around the globe! Are you ready to take off? Take off in your mind! Remember that choice is yours if you decide to fly in a commercial aircraft instead of a private jet!

88. Who told you that only birds with wings can fly? Look up to the sky and if you see an airplane, tell me or show me one person on that airplane that has wings, yet they are flying!

89. Don't confuse yourself that someday you will achieve your dreams. Begin to convince yourself that today is the day to achieve a little portion of your big dreams with the best of baby steps that you take. Have you taken any steps towards the actualization of your dreams today or are you waiting until one day or someday?

90. Do you have an immediate commandment that reminds you of your values or aspirations? A friend of mine who was on a diet repeatedly affirmed: "Thou shall not eat junk food but eat only healthily and work out at the gym faithfully."

91. Don't be a user of others but rather be useful unto others as you influence the world with your best thoughts, actions, inventions, and innovations! Useful people are successful people that get paid at the bank of life, in all currencies on the face of the earth!

92. Don't dwell in the city of mediocrity but take off with the velocity and tenacity for your grandest life, NOW!

93. It's an ageless proverb that the eagle and the chicken do not reside in the same territory. You belong to the association of flyers and not the club of grasshoppers! Move up! This is not discrimination but an inclination to move into the heights of greatness as you leave behind a company of heavyweight champions of endless idleness!

94. You cannot view the world through your lenses alone neither can you view the world through the news alone. Add books, travel, imagination, and observation to your lenses!

95. Inspiration is a virus that needs no vaccination but continuation!

96. To become assigned to your riches, you have to reach out to your assignment! To reach out to your assignment, you have to let go of your disappointment, then you have the freedom to embrace your appointment with open hands!

97. Aiming to win the lottery can be viewed as loitering around a field with billions of people and hoping that you are the lucky one who finds the golden coin. Why not use that same energy and faith in you that is waiting to win the lottery to generate an idea and begin to win your ideas instead of whining about winning the lottery! Play big on your ideas! Leave the lottery alone and stop loitering! The choice is yours!

If you decide to play the lottery one more time and you happen to win that million-dollar, send my share and forgive me for telling you to stop loitering in the lottery!

98. How are you influencing the world? "Influence is the only guaranteed **sure call** and not a **short cut** to becoming grand without waiting long to become a grandparent (my little joke)." On the other hand, you can become a **grandparent** (a parent that is grand), a **grandchild** (a child that is grand), a grand spouse, a grand friend, a grand teacher, a grand leader, a grand listener, a grand employee about to become a grand employer, a grand business owner, and grand in who you are and in all you do. You are grand! Just start with a grand attitude today!

99. There was a flower pot with flowers in it and I wondered if the flowers could become a flower field. A flower cannot transfer itself to a field but as a human being, you have the advantage to move your life into a bigger zone compared to a helpless flower. Ask yourself: "Am I a flower pot instead of being a flower field? Am I a plate of food instead of being a restaurant? Am I a gold necklace instead of being a gold mine? Am I a wallet or purse of money instead of being a bank? Am I a book instead of being a library? Am I a teacher instead of being a school?

Am I a doctor instead of being a hospital? Am I a clerk instead of being a CEO? Am I an airplane instead of being an airport? Am I a house instead of being an estate? Am I a recreation park instead of being a community? Am I a community instead of being a nation? Am I a nation instead of being the universe?

100. It's **TIME** to move from "Am I? to I AM!" The time is **NOW** to **WOW** the world with all the **POSSIBILITIES** inside of you!

Thank you for taking the time to scoop some soul food from this pot. Take it a step further by sharing it with another person so it can be multiplied.

Always remember that: "You were not called to be a "grain of sand" but to be a "beach full of sand" as you turn your ideas to wealth. You were not created to be a "bucket of water" but an "ocean of water" that fills the earth. You were not created to be "a handful of blessings" but to be "the world full of blessings" in this universe of humanity!"

OLATUNDE

www.ingramcontent.com/pod-product-compliance
Lightning Source LLC
Chambersburg PA
CBHW051235250726
48655CB00006B/2777